# Habitats

**by Arlene Block**

# What is a forest habitat?

Plants and animals live in a **habitat.**

A habitat gives shelter.

A habitat has what they need.

A **forest** is a habitat.

Animals live in a forest.

A forest has trees and plants.

# Forest Plants and Animals

It is summer.

Animals can get food.

Animals can get water.

Plants can get sun.

Plants can get water.

It is winter.

How did the forest change?

Plants get less sun.

Some trees drop their leaves.

It is hard for some animals to
find food.

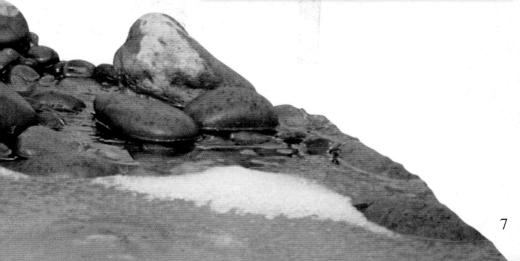

# What is a wetland habitat?

A **wetland** is a habitat.

A wetland is covered with water.

Animals live in a wetland.
Plants live in a wetland.
A wetland has what they need.

**Crane**

**Frog**

**Dragonfly**

# What is an ocean habitat?

An **ocean** is a habitat.

An ocean has salt water.

Plants live in an ocean.

Animals live in an ocean.

An ocean has what they need.

Sea turtle

Whale

Fish

# What is a desert habitat?

A **desert** is a habitat.

A desert is very dry.

A desert gets a lot of sun.

Plants and animals live in a desert.

This animal lives in a desert.

It needs very little water.

# Plants live in many habitats.

Animals live in many habitats.
Plants and animals get what they
need in their habitats.

# Glossary

**desert**    a habitat that is very dry

**forest**    a habitat that has many trees

**habitat**    a place where plants and animals live

**ocean**    a habitat that has salt water

**wetland**    a habitat that is covered with water